D1294302

ASK ABOUT

ASIA

Mason Crest Publishers Inc.
370 Reed Road, Broomall, Pennsylvania 19008
(866) MCP-BOOK (toll free)
www.masoncrest.com

13 12 11 10 09 08 07 06   10 9 8 7 6 5 4 3

Library of Congress Cataloging-in-Publication Data

Simpson, Judith.
  Indonesia / [text, Judith Simpson].
      p. cm. — (Ask about Asia)
Summary: Explores the geography, history, people, lifestyles, and
economy of Indonesia. Includes index.
      ISBN 1-59084-202-2
      ISBN 1-59084-198-0 (Series)
  1. Indonesia—Juvenile literature. [1. Indonesia.] I. Title. II.
Series.
DS615.S4985 2003
959.8—dc21   2004297189

Printed in Malaysia.

Original concept and production by Vineyard Freepress Pty Ltd,
Sydney.
Copyright © 1998

Project Editor	Valerie Hill
Text	Judith Simpson
Design	Denny Allnutt
Research	Peter Barker
Editor	Clare Booth
Cartography	Ray Sim
Consultants	Dorothy Minkoff, Alida Sijmons
Images	Garuda Indonesia, Annemarie Hollitzer, Holli Hollitzer, Pavel German, Indonesia Tourism Promotion Board, Consulate-General of the Republic of Indonesia, Reuters, Denny Allnutt, Valerie Hill, Allan Ashby, Allen Roberts.

COVER: *Legong* dancer, Bali.

TITLE PAGE: Cake decorated
with rice flour paste, Bali.

CONTENTS: Ploughing with
water buffalo, Sumatra.

INTRODUCTION: Senaru
children from Lombok.

Indonesia

MASON CREST PUBLISHERS

CONTENTS

THE LAND

GROWTH OF A NATION

WAR AND INDEPENDENCE

MODERN INDONESIA

DAILY LIFE

INTRODUCTION

INDONESIA is a string of islands stretching from the Indian to the Pacific Ocean. Four-fifths of the country's territory is water. Indonesia has a wide variety of ethnic groups. These groups are different in the way they look, their religious beliefs, the clothes they wear, their styles of houses and boats, their methods of agriculture, what they eat, and how they organize their society. They speak different languages, too, but most know Bahasa Indonesia, the language that unites the nation.

Indonesia has been independent for just over half a century. In this short time the country has had to adjust to the demands of the modern world. This book explores Indonesia's past and describes some of the changes and challenges facing Indonesian children today.

INDONESIA—TANAH AIR KITA

The 17,508 islands that make up the Indonesian archipelago are scattered across the Equator between the Asian mainland and Australia. Many of these islands are unnamed and only about 6,000 have people living on them. Indonesians call their country *Tanah Air Kita*, which means "our land and water." Sumatra, Java, Bali, Lombok, Komodo, and Timor are on the southern side of the chain of islands. To the north is Kalimantan—not an island in itself but part of Borneo. East of Kalimantan, the curious shape of Sulawesi has been likened to an orchid flower. The Maluku group was once called the Moluccas or the Spice Islands. The most eastern part of Indonesia, Irian Jaya, is joined to Papua New Guinea.

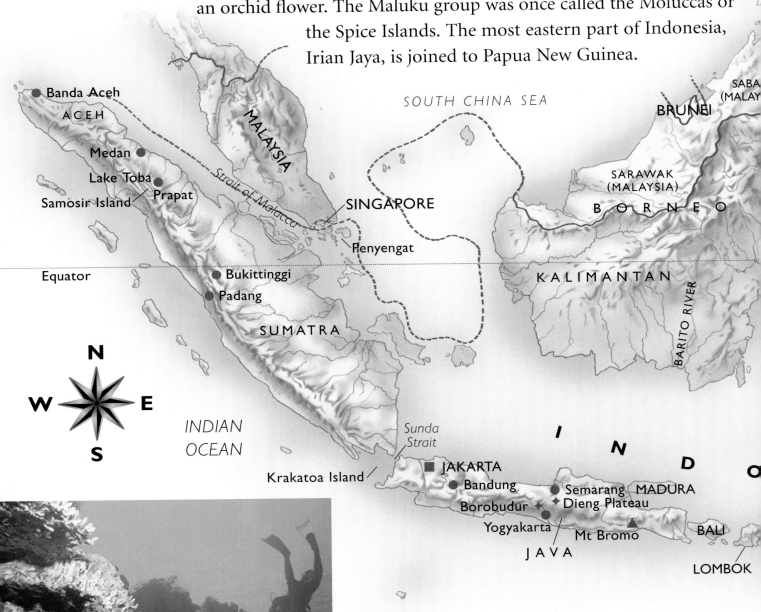

FACT FILE

Official Name: Republic of Indonesia
Official Language: Bahasa Indonesia
Population: 200,000,000, March 1997
Capital: Jakarta (Population: 12,000,000)
Currency: Rupiah (Rp)
Land Area: 741,101 sq miles (1,919,443 sq km)
Ethnic Groups: Javanese 40.1%; Sundanese 15.3%; Madurese 4.8%; Others 39.8%
Religions: Muslim 86.9%; Christian 9.6%; Hindu 1.9%; Buddhist 1.0%; Others 0.6%
Major Physical Features: Indonesia is the world's largest archipelago, made up of 17,508 islands. Highest mountain: Mount Jaya (Irian Jaya) 16,499 ft (5,029 m); Longest river: Barito (Kalimantan) 550 miles (885 km); Largest lake: Lake Toba (Sumatra) 685 sq miles (1,775 sq km)

CLIMATE

Most of the islands lie within the equatorial ever-wet zone and have two seasons, "the dry" and "the wet," which are determined by the monsoon winds that sweep across them. Monsoon rain falls in drenching sheets of warm water and there are often spectacular thunderstorms.

THE DRY (*musim kemarau*) March to August.
Drier winds from the southeast originate in Australia.
THE WET (*musim hujan*) September to February.
Winds from the northeast are laden with moisture after blowing across the South China Sea.

Every day of the year, the sun rises at about 6:00 a.m. and sets at about 6:00 p.m. The temperature at sea level is between 80° and 93°F (27° and 34°C) and the humidity is high. It is cooler further up the mountain slopes. The highest mountains in Irian Jaya are always capped with snow.

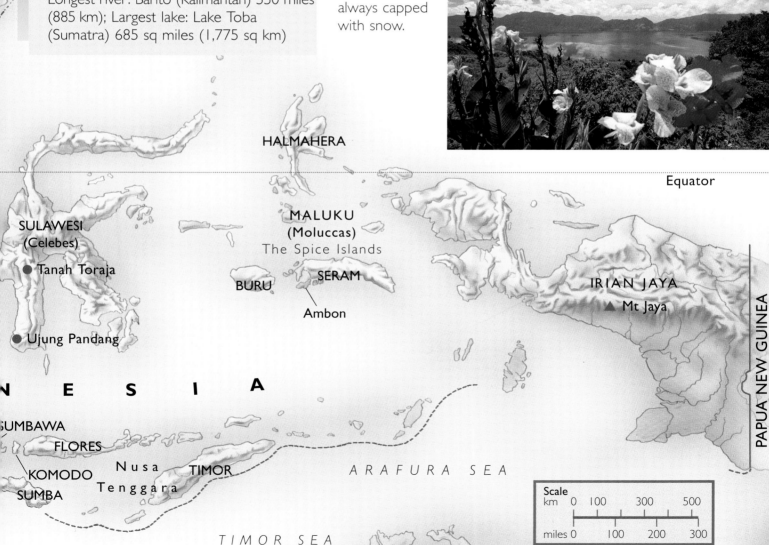

HALMAHERA

Equator

SULAWESI
(Celebes)

● Tanah Toraja

MALUKU
(Moluccas)
The Spice Islands

BURU

SERAM

Ambon

IRIAN JAYA

▲ Mt Jaya

● Ujung Pandang

N E S I A

PAPUA NEW GUINEA

SUMBAWA

FLORES

KOMODO

Nusa

TIMOR

Tenggara

SUMBA

A R A F U R A   S E A

Scale
km 0   100   300   500
miles 0   100   200   300

T I M O R   S E A

AUSTRALIA

A COUNTRY OF DIVERSITY

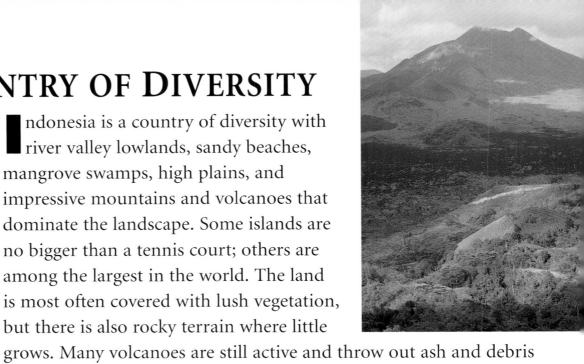

Indonesia is a country of diversity with river valley lowlands, sandy beaches, mangrove swamps, high plains, and impressive mountains and volcanoes that dominate the landscape. Some islands are no bigger than a tennis court; others are among the largest in the world. The land is most often covered with lush vegetation, but there is also rocky terrain where little grows. Many volcanoes are still active and throw out ash and debris from time to time. Volcanic debris comes in two kinds. Acid volcanic matter on many of the islands makes poor land for growing crops. But basic volcanic matter, which covers most of Java and Bali, produces fertile soil—people say that, in some places, a stick pushed into the ground will sprout leaves.

▲ Active volcanoes smoke and steam. According to legend, an ogre used a coconut shell to dig one of Java's huge volcanic craters in a single night.

VOLCANIC ACTION

Erupting volcanoes have the power to change the face of the landscape and fill the earth's atmosphere with debris that blocks out the sun. Lake Toba on Sumatra is the result of an enormous volcanic explosion that happened in prehistoric times. The crater it left behind filled with water to make a huge, deep lake. Today, Lake Toba is a peaceful place with no hint of volcanic activity. Krakatoa, near Sumatra, blew up in 1883, destroying most of the island it was on. The explosion was heard as far away as Colombo in Sri Lanka and Sydney in Australia.

◄ Nowhere in Indonesia are you ever far from an active volcano.

Say it in
BAHASA INDONESIA!
Island—*pulau* (Pulau Komodo)
Lake—*danau* (Danau Toba)
Mountain—*gunung* (Gunung Bromo)
River—*sungai* (Sungai Barito)

About 300 ethnic groups live in Indonesia speaking more than 580 languages and dialects. Communities follow their own ways of doing things. The differences are great between, for example, a Batak family on North Sumatra, a family from Java, and a Dayak family living in a longhouse on Kalimantan.

▲ Batak woman and baby from Sumatra.

▶ This woman and child from Java are Muslims like many other Javans.

Island	Area of land (square miles)	Number of people (from 1990 census)
Bali	2,169	2.8 million
Java	51,553	107.6 million
Sulawesi	73,794	12.5 million
Irian Jaya	164,573	1.7 million
Sumatra	184,706	36.6 million
Kalimantan	210,405	9.1 million

▲ This table gives you more information about some areas named on the map on pages 8 and 9. The table shows the size of the area and the number of people living there. From these figures, you can see that some parts of Indonesia are more crowded than others. Java has by far the greatest number of inhabitants, but it is not the largest area of land. About 60 percent of Indonesia's total population live on Java—more than 312 people per square mile.

▲ Dayak people in Kalimantan live in longhouses with many families sharing each one.

◀ The Batak people around Lake Toba used wooden pegs and wedges instead of nails when they built their traditional houses.

ANIMALS AND PLANTS

Indonesia supports a great variety of wildlife. For example, there are 21 types of monkeys and apes in Kalimantan. Coral, seaweeds, dazzling tropical fish, and other creatures thrive in seas off the islands, although pollution in some areas is reducing numbers. Animals of western Indonesia, such as elephants, clouded leopards, and reticulated pythons, are found in Asia. Animals of the east, in Irian Jaya and nearby islands, are similar to Australian species and include possum-like cuscuses, kangaroos, bandicoots, and spiny anteaters. Like wildlife in other parts of the world, the future of Indonesia's animals and plants depends on what humans do to the environment in which they live.

▲ The reticulated python squeezes its prey to death in its strong coils. These snakes may grow up to 33 feet (10 m) long.

▶ The more fertile parts of Indonesia are a natural garden for thousands of flowering plant species.

◀ Cassowaries are large heavy birds that cannot fly. They live in Irian Jaya and neighboring islands and eat fallen fruits and insects from the rainforest floor. Cassowaries have glossy black plumage.

▲ The common spotted cuscus searches trees for leaves and fruit. From time to time it also eats small lizards or baby birds.

UNIQUE AND ENDANGERED

Shaggy, long-armed orangutans (orang-utan means "man of the jungle"), found wild only in Borneo and northern Sumatra, are becoming fewer and are classified as an endangered species. An even rarer mammal, the one-horned Javan rhinoceros, which lives nowhere else in the world, is close to extinction—in 1997, no more than 75 were thought to be still alive. Birds are battling for survival, too—the Bali starling is just one listed for conservation.

PLANT DIVERSITY. Known species of Indonesian plants outnumber the total plant species of Africa or America, and many have yet to be identified. Orchids, including a black one, grow in abundance. There are about 250 different kinds of bamboo and 150 species of palm trees. The rafflesia has no leaves but its flower is three feet (one meter) across. Plants grow in water as well as on land.

◀ Pitcher plants digest insects trapped in their liquid-filled cups.

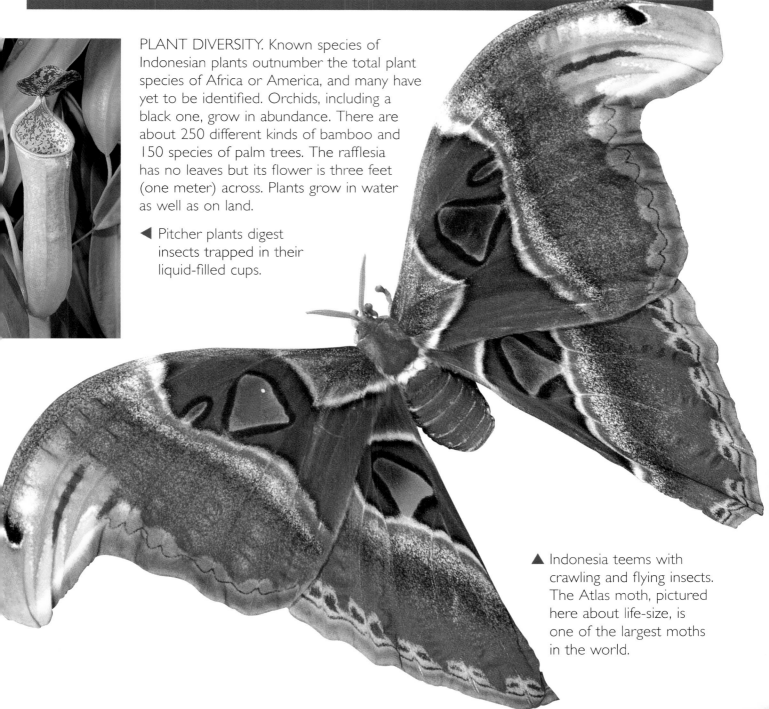

▲ Indonesia teems with crawling and flying insects. The Atlas moth, pictured here about life-size, is one of the largest moths in the world.

THE FIRST SETTLERS

People have lived on the chain of islands now called Indonesia from early prehistoric times. The ancestors of most modern Indonesians, however, began settling there less than 4,500 years ago, forcing the original inhabitants into the isolated places where their descendants live today. From around 2500 BC onward, groups migrated from Vietnam and southern China. They brought their tools and technology with them, and built villages and boats and raised crops. Some grew rice in flooded fields, a method that farmers still use today.

▲ Indonesian from Nusa Tenggara.

▼ Wet rice cultivation.

▲ Indonesian from South Sulawesi.

▼ Dugout canoe on Lake Toba, Sumatra.

Early communities lived up and down the rivers, beside lakes, and along the coasts of some of the islands. Sometimes rival groups fought each other. Villagers developed different languages, family behavior and ways of celebrating important events. Their religious rituals reflected their belief in "animism." Their social customs depended on the *adat* of the group.

▲ Asmat ceremonial dancer from Irian Jaya.

ANIMISM AND ADAT

People believed that natural objects such as mountains, trees, animals, rice, rain, and the sun had spirits that controlled everything that happened—storms, growth of crops, sickness, or other events. These beliefs are called "animism." Statues, totem poles, masks, dances, and ceremonial clothing served the multitude of spirits. Many groups also worshiped their ancestors. Later, when new religions came from other countries—Hinduism and Buddhism from India, Islam from Saudi Arabia, Christianity from Europe—people blended them with their old beliefs.

The customs and laws that Indonesians live by are called *adat*. Rules of behavior, passed from one generation to another, cover matters such as inheritance; birth, marriage, and death ceremonies; courtship; cooking and eating.

▲▼ BARONG MASKS
These modern Balinese masks represent an ancient story. Dancers often perform the legend of the courageous lion-like Barong defeating Ranga (below), the wicked queen of the witches. This dance is intended to drive away evil spirits.

The Indonesians have a saying, "Religion comes in from the sea, but customs come down from the mountains." The new religions brought in by sailing ships frequently exist in harmony with traditional *adat*.

◀ Totem poles for protection still stand in Kalimantan.

THE AGE OF EMPIRES

Many kingdoms rose and fell in Indonesia during the Age of Empires. Some were small groups of villages; others were vast territories. During this time Indian traders, wandering Buddhist monks, and Brahman priests brought knowledge of Buddhism and Hinduism to the islands. The local rulers began following these religions, but little remains of their empires except the religious ideas and some stone temples. At the end of the seventh century, kings of the Buddhist empire of Sriwijaya in South Sumatra controlled the passage of ships through the Malacca and Sunda Straits. For 600 years Sriwijaya survived on trade; it produced little itself and even had to import rice.

▲
Temples on the Dieng Plateau— "the place of the ancestors." The oldest temples in Indonesia blend belief in the importance of ancestor spirits with new religions.

SAILING SKILLS

Guided by the stars alone, the sailors of Sulawesi have traded in the waters of the archipelago for centuries in schooners built by their own boatbuilders. These days the schooners are equipped with engines.

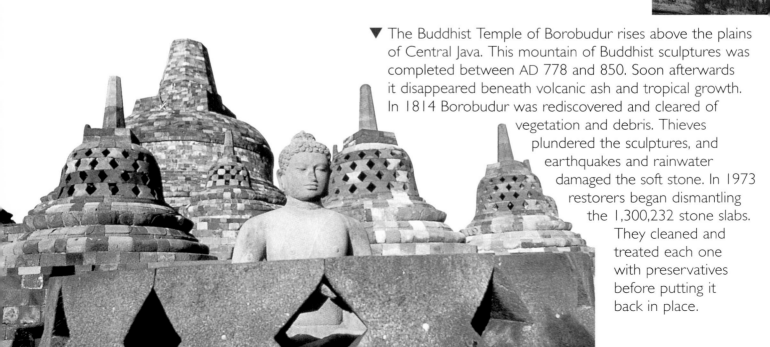

▼ The Buddhist Temple of Borobudur rises above the plains of Central Java. This mountain of Buddhist sculptures was completed between AD 778 and 850. Soon afterwards it disappeared beneath volcanic ash and tropical growth. In 1814 Borobudur was rediscovered and cleared of vegetation and debris. Thieves plundered the sculptures, and earthquakes and rainwater damaged the soft stone. In 1973 restorers began dismantling the 1,300,232 stone slabs. They cleaned and treated each one with preservatives before putting it back in place.

The Hindu empire of Majapahit began in East Java in 1294. It reached the height of its power in the fourteenth century when it extended from Sumatra to Maluku, covering much of what is now modern Indonesia. It relied on wet rice cultivation, control of trade routes, and tribute from conquered states. Majapahit's success in uniting Indonesia as one empire inspired later rulers.

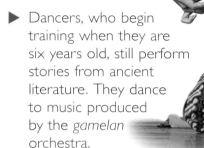

▶ Dancers, who begin training when they are six years old, still perform stories from ancient literature. They dance to music produced by the *gamelan* orchestra.

▲ Loro Jonggrang Temple, Prambanan. Sculptures on some of the walls of this ninth-century Hindu temple depict scenes from the *Ramayana*, an ancient Indian story poem adopted by Indonesian rulers.

▼ This book illustrates scenes from the *Ramayana*. The book is made of dried lontar palm leaves.

▲ Gongs, cymbals, drums, xylophones, and other instruments form the *gamelan*. Several *gamelan* systems are played in the archipelago —some are lively, others are slow and stately.

THE COMING OF ISLAM

Arab merchants had long been trading in South East Asia. They introduced the religion of Islam, based on the teachings of the prophet Mohammed, to Sumatra. Many Sumatrans were converted to the new faith. Being part of Islam not only gave the coastal Sumatrans a new religion, it also secured them a place in the Islamic trade network. This network stretched from Arabia to North Africa and across the Indian Ocean to India and South East Asia.

▼ Muslims worship in buildings called mosques. From them, *muezzins* (criers) call the faithful to prayer, their voices ringing out through loudspeakers.

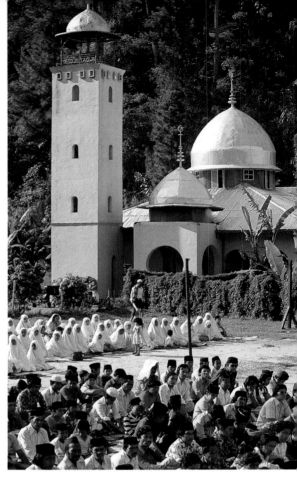

▲ There are many mosques, or *mesjids*, on the Indonesian islands. Men and women must be seated and pray in separate spaces.

THE ISLAMIC RELIGION

During the seventh century AD the prophet Mohammed founded the religion of Islam in Saudi Arabia. Followers of Mohammed, called Muslims, began spreading his teachings throughout the world. The *Koran* is regarded by the faithful as the word of God. The man who leads the congregation in prayer in a mosque is called an *imam*. Muslims' religious duties include praying daily, giving money to the poor, and keeping certain rules such as not eating pork. During the month of Ramadan Muslims fast from before dawn until after sunset.

▶ *Imams* read daily from the *Koran*.

The Islamic faith spread from Sumatra to other islands. In the early sixteenth century, the Islamic kingdom of Demak in Sumatra conquered the last great Hindu kingdom of Java. Its rulers fled to

Bali. Present-day Indonesia has the largest Muslim population of any country in the world, but most people in Bali still practice a form of Hinduism.

◄ The Istiqlal mosque in Jakarta is Indonesia's largest mosque. The first stone was laid by President Sukarno on 24 August 1961.

▲ This Muslim boy, dressed as a prince, is taking part in a ceremony that marks the end of childhood for boys between 11 and 12 years old.

▼ Muslim women who are strict about their religion cover their heads when they leave the privacy of their homes.

▲ The traditional buildings of the Minangkabau, a devoutly Muslim community in West Sumatra, indicate great wealth. It is the Minangkabau women, however, who own and inherit family property, and whose names and titles are passed on. This is unusual in Islamic society, which generally focuses on men.

EUROPE IN CONTROL

European traders came looking for cloves and nutmegs in the Spice Islands (Maluku). These fetched high prices in Europe, where they were used for flavoring and preserving meat. During the sixteenth century the Portuguese traded actively in Indonesia and established the Catholic religion. The first ships from Holland arrived in 1596. In 1602 the newly formed Dutch East India Company (VOC) began to take over the Indonesian islands. The VOC went bankrupt in 1799 but Dutch colonial rule continued, almost unbroken, into the twentieth century. The Dutch made money from introduced crops such as rubber, tobacco, tea, and coffee, and expanded sugar cane cultivation in Java. Peasant laborers on the plantations received tiny wages and landowners paid high taxes to the government. The Dutch and Indonesians fought bitter battles for control of land.

▲ From 1839 the harbor master's watchtower and cannon guarded Batavia's port. Indonesia's flag flies outside the building, which is now part museum, part police station.

▶ Portuguese trade ship.

THE SPICE TRADE

The Spice Islands were once the only place where cloves and nutmegs grew. Hundreds of years before Europeans reached their shores, traders had taken cloves from them to the Chinese court, where courtiers chewed them to sweeten their breath before seeing the emperor. The VOC tried to keep the spice trade for themselves, but plants were smuggled out and grown successfully elsewhere.

▲ Drying cloves in Central Java.

▶ Model, made from cloves, of a sailing ship that carried spices to Europe.

BATAVIA

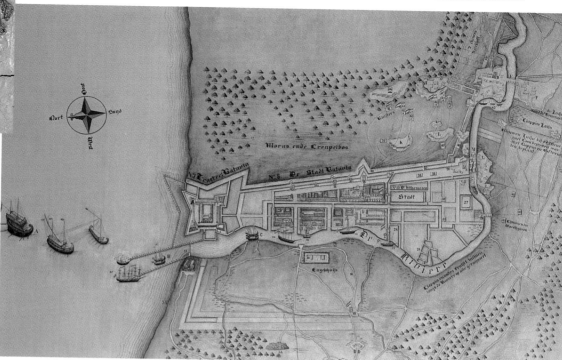

▶ The Dutch burned the old Javan town of Jayakarta in 1619 and built a new town, called Batavia, in its place. Batavia became the Dutch headquarters in Indonesia. It is now the historical area of Jakarta. The Dutch built houses like those at home in Holland and even dug canals for transporting goods. You can see the canals clearly on this seventeenth-century map of Batavia.

◀ The Dutch East India Company was known by its initials—VOC. They stood for the company's name in Dutch—Vereenigde Oost-Indische Compagnie. The Indonesian islands became the Dutch East Indies.

▶ In the late nineteenth century the Dutch began building railway lines to replace horsedrawn transport in Java.

▼ Dutch buildings at Fort Rotterdam in Ujung Padang in South Sulawesi.

◀ The statue of Martha Christina Tiahahu gazes across Ambon Bay. She was one of many who resisted the Dutch. After Martha was captured, she starved herself to death on the way to exile in Java.

▲ Two colors—red standing for courage and white representing purity—have been linked with Indonesia since the thirteenth century. The flag, which has been in use since the 1920s, became the nation's official emblem after World War II.

▼ Modern road builders know how difficult it is to build and maintain permanent tracks in this country of mountains, rivers, swamps, and heavy rainfall.

THE STRUGGLE FOR INDEPENDENCE

By 1910 the Dutch firmly controlled the whole archipelago, except for East Timor, but the wealth gained from oil and other products benefited Holland rather than the Dutch East Indies. The Dutch did little for the local people, except for educating a few students from upper-class families. One of the students, called Sukarno, became a leader of those Indonesians who wanted *merdeka* (freedom) from colonial rule. During World War II, from March 1942, the Japanese army occupied the Dutch East Indies. These were tough years for the Indonesians. The Japanese, however, encouraged the use of Bahasa Indonesia as a common language, which helped to spread ideas about independence. When the Japanese surrendered to the Americans on 14 August 1945, Sukarno and Hatta had become Indonesia's nationalist leaders. On 17 August, they declared the country independent and free from the rule of other nations.

▼ With the arrival of motor cars, the Dutch built roads in Java, which now has the nation's best transport system and the largest share of its roads.

▲ It is not surprising that after more than three centuries of occupation Dutch influences, such as this streetlamp, can still be seen throughout Indonesia.

Sukarno became the first president of Indonesia. (In Indonesia important people are often known by a single name.) He drew up the Republic of Indonesia's constitution based on the *Pancasila*, which means "five principles" (see page 26). Sukarno turned to China and Russia as allies during his term of office.

JAPANESE OCCUPATION

During World War II, the Japanese took all Indonesia's raw materials. These included oil, rubber, rice, and spices. People had to give up their gold jewelry and gemstones. Many objects made of wrought iron, such as gates and railings, were shipped to Japan to be melted down to make weapons and tanks.

BAHASA INDONESIA

Indonesia's official language, Bahasa Indonesia, is a symbol of nationhood and a way of unifying the people. However, not all Indonesians speak the national language. People in remote regions may be poorly educated. They do not travel far and have little need to know any other than their local language. In most villages, there is someone who can speak Bahasa Indonesia.

Greetings in
BAHASA INDONESIA
Selamat—Congratulations / good luck / good health
Selamat pagi—Good morning
Selamat siang—Good afternoon
Selamat malam—Good night
Selamat berjalan—Have a good trip

Bahasa Indonesia gives the people a shared tongue. National newspapers are printed in Bahasa Indonesia. National radio and television are presented in Bahasa Indonesia. People speak Bahasa Indonesia in Indonesian movies, and foreign films have Bahasa Indonesia subtitles.

Bahasa Indonesia is related to the Malay tongue, but has taken many words from other languages such as Arabic, Sanskrit (an ancient Indian language), English, French, Portuguese, Spanish, and Dutch. Like English and other European languages, Bahasa Indonesia is written in the Roman alphabet.

MERDEKA! FREEDOM!

The Indonesians rejoiced with cries of *"Merdeka!"* ("Freedom!") in 1945, but then the Dutch returned. It was not until December 1949 that Indonesia was finally left to govern itself. There were many difficulties. Factories and plantations had been closed or destroyed. The country lacked money and educated people to run the government. There was too little rice to feed the growing population. After a troubled period, President Sukarno introduced martial law, which meant he depended on the army to support him. In October 1965, a group of dissatisfied army officers tried to seize power. Mob violence followed and many people were killed or imprisoned. General Suharto restored order and acted as president until he was officially elected in 1968. The 1970s and 1980s were years of development for Indonesia. In the 1990s too much power and wealth became concentrated in the hands of too few.

◀ General Suharto became Indonesia's second president. His presidency lasted until May 1998 when he was forced to resign.

▼ Merdeka Day, celebrated on 17 August, is a national holiday for Indonesians.

▲ This monument is a tribute to the six generals and one army officer who were assassinated on 1 October 1965. It stands in the center of a memorial park in Jakarta, near the old well into which the men's bodies had been thrown. Earlier, Sukarno had named 1965 "the Year of Living Dangerously."

THE CRAFT TRADITION

Village craftspeople work in wood, clay, and other materials, using simple tools. The leather shadow puppets of Java, called *wayang kulit*, were first used in rituals to ward off evil spirits. As Indonesia changed so did the puppets, and in the last five centuries *wayang kulit* stories have blended religious beliefs. The puppet shows have also encouraged thoughts about freedom from colonialism and the principles of independence. The audience sees only silhouettes when the puppets are held up to a screen lit from behind. Shows, backed by *gamelan* music, last all night.

GOVERNING 17,508 ISLANDS

Unified government is difficult to achieve in Indonesia because the islands are spread across 3,100 miles (5,000 km) of ocean and there are so many different ethnic groups.

The *garuda* on the Indonesian coat of arms holds a banner bearing the words *Bhinneka Tunggal Ika*, which mean "unity in diversity" or "we are many but we are one." Some Indonesians do not support the central government's attempts to create a national identity. These people say that if the government tries too hard for unity, diversity will disappear. They fear local customs will be lost forever. Feelings against government policies are strongest in Aceh in northern Sumatra; in Irian Jaya, which remained under Dutch control until 1962; and in East Timor, which was Portuguese until 1975.

▲
The *garuda* is a golden eagle that appears in ancient Indonesian and Malaysian folk tales. *Garudas* turn up all over Indonesia. This one is made of carved and painted wood.

THE INDONESIAN CONSTITUTION

Five symbols on the coat of arms represent the five principles of Indonesia's constitution—the *Pancasila*. These *silas* state:

Star (first *sila*; center): Belief in the One and Only God

Chain (second *sila*; lower right): Just and Civilized Humanity

Banyan tree (third *sila*; upper right): The Unity of Indonesia

Water buffalo (fourth *sila*; upper left): Democracy Guided by the Inner Wisdom in the Unanimity Arising out of Deliberations Among Representatives

Rice and cotton plants (fifth *sila*; lower left): Social Justice for the Whole of the People of Indonesia.

The *Pancasila* sets out a way of life for Indonesia's millions. School and university students, government employees, and people in government-related jobs attend courses to learn about the *Pancasila*.

▶ THE LEVELS OF GOVERNMENT
To manage the vast spread of Indonesia, the country is divided into 27 provinces, each with a a capital city and a governor. Provinces are divided into districts. Districts contain towns and villages.

STATE
President

PROVINCE
Governor

DISTRICT
Bupati (Regent)

TOWN
Walikota (Mayor)

VILLAGE
Village Head and Council of Elders

▲ The business of the district is done in an office building.

▶ Making decisions at the village level means long hours of discussion until agreement is reached on a matter. This man is the head of a Dayak longhouse on Kalimantan. A Dayak headman usually lives in the center of a longhouse. He is responsible for handling the community's affairs.

▲ The Indonesian constitution allows people to choose their religion. This Chinese temple is in Semarang in Central Java, where almost half the population is Chinese.

▶ In March 1998, Suharto began his seventh five-year term as president. Most Indonesians were unhappy with the election results. In May 1998, this photograph appeared in newspapers around the world. It showed thousands of students outside the Indonesian parliament in Jakarta. They are calling for Suharto to go. He finally resigned on 22 May 1998. Dr. Habibie took his place.

INDONESIA AND OTHER COUNTRIES

Indonesia has strong contacts with other Asian countries and the rest of the world on matters of trade, manufacturing, foreign affairs and education. Indonesians receive grants to study abroad. Foreign teachers and education equipment are sent to Indonesia. Visiting engineers work with Indonesian engineers on designs for roads, bridges, and dams. Experts from other countries give advice to Indonesian farmers. They have helped to control disease in water buffalo and to select suitable fertilizers for soil conditions of the archipelago. Indonesia also takes part in international sporting events. At the Asian Games, Indonesians compete in badminton, martial arts, soccer, swimming, and table tennis. In 1992, when badminton first became an Olympic sport, Indonesians won five medals.

▲ Indonesian naval cadets learn to rig tall ships. They sail two of these vessels on goodwill visits to other countries and compete in tall ship races.

▲ Indonesia's money unit is called the rupiah. There are coins as well as banknotes. When times are troubled, prices rise. Rupiahs buy less food and other goods than before. In bad times, rupiahs are not worth as much when they are exchanged for foreign money such as American dollars, Japanese yen, or British pounds.

▶ Most of the world learns about what is happening in Indonesia from newspaper reports and radio and television programs. This picture shows villagers in central Sumatra in February 1998 fighting fires started by land clearing. Light monsoon rains had left the forests unusually dry.

▲ Some people in other countries like to cook Indonesian recipes. The ingredients you can see in this container are *laos* (a dried root with a peppery gingery flavor); *kemiri* (candle nuts), which are often served with curries; turmeric (a yellow powdered root used to color food) and star anise, which tastes like sweet licorice.

INTERNATIONAL VISITORS

Tourism is expected to be increasingly important in Indonesia in the twenty-first century. Two difficult tasks will be providing enough hotels and services for tourists, and preserving the unique things that make people want to visit the country.

▲ Nusa Dua, a resort on Bali.

Indonesia has more than one world-class center where conferences can be held. The assembly hall in Jakarta's Convention Centre seats 4,000 people and there is space for exhibitions. In 1994, Jakarta hosted the Asia Pacific Economic Cooperation (APEC) group's summit meeting. The government hopes that more events of this kind will take place in Indonesia.

◄ A large hall in Jakarta's modern Convention Centre is equipped with video display screens.

▼ Dancers from the Ekayana Dance Studio make international tours. These performances give foreign audiences a chance to see traditional Javanese dances.

▲ This boy has had an eye operation. Indonesian specialist doctors, such as eye surgeons, usually train in overseas hospitals and return to their country to practice.

FROM LAND AND SEA

▼ Traditionally, the ripe rice stalks are cut with a tiny sickle hidden in the hand so that Dewi Sri, the rice goddess, is not startled.

More than 60 percent of Indonesians work the land. They grow rice, corn, cassava, sweet potatoes, sago, and vegetables, or tend plantation crops such as coffee and oil palms. Farmers flood fertile level ground or terraced hillsides for wet rice cultivation. They enclose these rice fields with earth walls and control the supply of water from irrigation channels. Bali's rich soil produces two or three crops a year. In drier areas, farmers slash and burn to clear land for planting. After a couple of seasons, they move on to clear more ground, leaving the used earth to recover its nutrients. Natural disasters—torrential monsoon rains or forest fires such as those of 1997 and 1998— sometimes destroy large areas of land. Fishing and fish farming are important pursuits.

▲ Coconut palms have grown here from prehistoric times. Indonesia exports shredded coconut for use in cakes and confectionery, and coconut oil to add to soap and margarine. The coconut husk produces fiber called coir. It is made into ropes and matting.

◄ Few Indonesian farmers own tractors. Instead they use water buffalo to pull their ploughs.

► Farmers rear cattle, sheep, goats and poultry. Everyone in the family who is old enough and fit enough shares the work.

◄ Tea is one of the successful plantation crops introduced by the Dutch. Indonesia exports tea to other countries.

A FISHY PROBLEM

Fish supply valuable protein in the Indonesian diet. Traditional fishing methods, such as the one shown here, use small nets restricting the numbers of fish that can be caught. Modern vessels with electronic fish finders and big nets are replacing these methods. If too many fish are caught, they will stop breeding, and there will be no more for the future. How can this problem be solved?

INDUSTRY AND THE ECONOMY

To help pay for health care, education, transport and communication systems, defense, and other services, the government exchanges raw materials and manufactured goods for money or products Indonesia needs from other countries. Indonesia's natural resources include oil and liquid natural gas, coal, tin, bauxite, copper, gold, silver, and timber. The country also sells plantation crops and has a thriving tourist industry. Ancient village crafts—basket making, pottery, metal working, wood and stone carving, weaving, and puppet making—are minor exports. Since 1980, there has been steady growth in the number of factories producing manufactured goods. International businesses have built factories in Indonesia, where workers' wages are low. Despite rapid industrial development, the country still depends on financial aid from overseas to balance its expenses. In the late 1990s, Indonesia's economy was in turmoil and contributors were questioning how their aid money was being spent.

▲ This quarry is near Bandung in West Java. Limestone is used within Indonesia in the building trade.

▼ Indonesia is the world's largest producer of liquid natural gas and exports large amounts to Japan, Taiwan, and South Korea.

◀ ▲ Indonesia's forests provide timber and bamboo. Some forest plants are being researched as sources of medicine. In many places regrowth trees are planted to replace those felled but the Indonesian rainforest has taken so long to grow that it would take centuries to restore it to its original state after clearing.

TEXTILES

Ikat weaving is an ancient village craft, practiced on certain islands in the Nusa Tenggara group. Weavers use natural dyes made from leaves, roots, and bark to color the threads, which they weave into traditional designs on simple looms. The best pieces of *ikat* fetch high prices in art galleries overseas.

The making of *batik* fabric, the best-known Indonesian craft, is thought to have begun in Java. Traditional *batik* makers apply melted beeswax to cloth from a small container called a *canting*. They apply the wax in a planned design. When the waxed cloth is dipped in the dyeing vat, the waxed areas resist the color. After the first dyeing, the *batik* makers scrape away the wax, apply more wax in a new design, and dip the cloth in a second color. They repeat this process until the full design is finished in several colors. A newer, quicker method of producing *batik* is now also used.

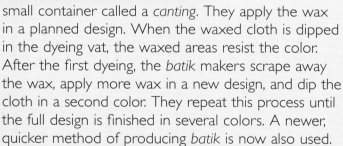

▲ Rubber is one of the most successful plantation crops introduced by the Dutch. Indonesia exports rubber and products made from rubber. Tapping means cutting the rubber trees so that the sap can ▼ trickle into a bowl.

▲▼
Like so many capital cities throughout the world, Jakarta's main streets are never free from motor vehicles. In peak hours, traffic slows to a snail's pace, sending choking petrol fumes into the hot, steamy air. Three-wheeled taxis crawl forward between weaving motor cycles and the latest-model foreign cars. Indonesian motorists accept traffic jams as a part of city life.

JAKARTA—IBU KOTA

The capital of Indonesia, Jakarta, is also called *Ibu Kota* meaning "Mother City." It is a city of contrasts. Here are Indonesia's most expensive apartment blocks as well as cardboard hovels that house the very poor. Here are multilane highways and narrow, grimy alleyways. Here are profitable Western-style department stores and street-side pedlars barely making a living.

▲ The region first settled by the Dutch is known as *Kota* or Old Batavia. Batavia's Town Hall, built in 1707, is now the Jakarta Museum of History.

◄ The National Monument, known as Monas, stands in the middle of Merdeka Square. It commemorates Independence Day, 17 August 1945.

◀ *Taman Mini Indonesia Indah* (Beautiful Indonesia in Miniature), 6 miles (10 km) from Jakarta, brings together the Indonesian cultures. The 27 pavilions—one for each of the provinces—display crafts, traditional costumes, musical instruments, and other things illustrating life in the region. The walk-in bird enclosure at *Taman Mini* houses native birds in their natural surroundings.

▶ Jaya Ancol Dreamland is a modern recreation park for tourists and Jakartans alike, especially the younger ones.

The city center contains government buildings, air-conditioned office skyscrapers, first-class hotels, and impressive monuments. In the suburbs one- and two-story structures are mixed. Shops, offices, and factories are set among people's homes, which grew up in *kampung*, or village, style after World War II, when people from the country flocked to live in the cities.

▶ Caged birds are expensive at Jakarta's bird market and only the rich can afford them. Owners train birds to take part in singing competitions.

▲ This bronze statue commemorates Prince Diponegoro, who was the eldest son of a Javanese sultan. In the nineteenth century the prince led a five-year resistance movement against the Dutch.

▶ Ocean-going, handmade, wooden schooners still deliver cargoes to Sunda Kelapa, Jakarta's harbor area. Once a Hindu spice-trading port, Sunda Kelapa was conquered and converted to Islam more than 450 years ago.

BEING INDONESIAN

Indonesians are brought up to care for others. They are encouraged to think of the family, local community and society as a whole. They tend to follow group customs and behave in a similar manner but individuality, Western-style, is becoming more common among younger people. Indonesians do not expect to have much personal privacy—they share their feelings, their possessions, their space, their time, and their business. Honor and respect for elders and not "losing face"—or being embarrassed—are still important in Indonesian society. Indonesians value good manners and show guests great generosity. The pace of life is leisurely—most live by *jam karet*, which means "rubber time."

▲ Being Indonesian means taking pots to market on Lombok.

► Being Indonesian means bargaining over the price of ducks at a Javan market.

◄ Being Indonesian means measuring wealth in water buffalo horns

► . . . and making effigies of the dead to serve the worship of the ancestors in Tanah Toraja on South Sulawesi.

▲ Being Indonesian means taking
shelter from rain on Lombok

◄ . . . or taking part in a religious
procession in East Java.

Say it in
BAHASA INDONESIA
Apa kabar?—How are you?
Saya mengerti—I understand.
Saya kurang mengerti—I don't
understand.
Terima kasih—Thank you.

▲ Being Indonesian means
praying at the mosque on
the small island of Penyengat.

◄ Being Indonesian means carrying
passionfruit to a Bali market

▼ . . . or making music on
bamboo *angklungs* in West Java.

▲ Being Indonesian means
playing chess in a Sanur
street on Bali.

FAMILY MATTERS

Family ties and loyalties are strong. In Indonesia, parents, children, grandparents, grandchildren, aunts, uncles, and cousins may all live together in one house. Family members who go out to work contribute to household expenses. During the holiday that marks the end of Ramadan, absent family members return home to celebrate and swap news. Traditional respect for parents—especially the father, or *bapak*—still exists at the village level. However, the middle classes and well educated are becoming more independent and individual under the influences of Western television, computer networking, and travel. In particular, young girls and women are now increasingly free.

▼ The community welcomes a new baby with rituals, feasting, and prayers for strength and good health. For a year, at least, babies live safely in a cloth sling attached to their mothers, aunts, or older sisters. This is most important in Indonesia where diseases still kill many infants.

▶ Young children are watched over carefully to see that they come to no harm. There is always someone in the family who will play with them or hold them.

WATER AND WASHING
Washing in lakes or rivers means a chance to chat with neighbors. In some villages, water has to be fetched daily for drinking, cooking, and washing clothes and people.

REDUCING THE NUMBERS
The government encourages people to have fewer children. This will slow down the rate at which the population is growing. A five-rupiah coin once showed a couple with two children—the message was "Two is enough." One way of dealing with overcrowding in some islands is to move families from one island to another. These families receive a plot of land, a house, a supply of food, basic farming tools and seeds to start them off in their new homes. This policy, first begun in 1904 by the Dutch, is called transmigration. It is not popular.

▼ ▶
When an Indonesian dies, family and friends gather to honor the deceased. Funeral arrangements vary according to the ethnic group. The Hindu Balinese cremate their dead in a tower in the shape of a mythical beast. They believe that burning the body frees the soul to journey to heaven.

▲ Indonesians of different regions have different marriage ceremonies. The bride and bridegroom, such as this couple from Lombok, dress in elaborate clothes. Many guests come to wish them luck.

FOOD FROM ALL REGIONS

Steamed white rice, served with side dishes of vegetables, fish, chicken, or meat, usually forms the main part of Indonesian meals. On some islands the people's basic diet consists of corn, sago, cassava, or sweet potatoes. Many dishes are made with coconut or coconut milk and flavored with herbs, spices, and hot chillies.

Chinese, Indian, Arab, Portuguese, and Dutch tastes have all influenced Indonesian cooking. Different regions have special dishes or ways of preparing food. Some Indonesians eat dogs, monkeys, mice, lizards, and bats, and non-Muslims enjoy pork. In North Maluku, yellow saffron-flavored rice is served with *sate* and curry. In West Sumatra the famous Padang cookery is extra hot and spicy.

▲ Garlic, chili and ginger make Indonesian food tasty.

▼ Food vendors gather in open-air markets or sell tasty snacks from roadside stalls. Pieces of meat are grilled on skewers over a charcoal fire.

TABLE MANNERS

- The custom in Indonesia is to eat with your fingers rather than with cutlery. Use the right hand only—the left hand is considered unclean.
- Indonesians prefer to eat sitting down. They joke, "*Makannya seperti kuda*—Eating like horses!" (meaning, standing up).
- The host starts eating, then everyone can begin.
- Leave food on your plate when you have finished—a clean plate means you want more.

FAVORITE FOODS

Nasi goreng—fried rice with pieces of egg, meat, fish, and vegetables

Mie goreng—fried noodles combined with pieces of egg, meat, fish, and vegetables

Gado-gado—cooked vegetable salad with peanut sauce

Sate—grilled meat on a skewer

◀ Indonesia's fruit trees bear many different kinds of tropical and subtropical fruits—some native to the islands, others grown from imported stock. This picture shows *jamba* (guavas), star fruit, *manggis*, bananas, and, in the front on the left, a type of orange that is ripe when it is green.

▶ Stallholders in the food markets usually wrap purchases in banana leaves instead of paper.

▲ Indonesians prefer seafood, poultry, and eggs to red meat. Fresh fish are often for sale in the markets.

◀ The durian is a large tropical fruit with a rough skin and white creamy flesh. People say it "tastes like heaven and smells like hell." It smells so bad, it is banned from some public places, on airplanes, and in hotel rooms.

▲ ▶
Small packages of food, beautifully prepared, are presented daily to Bali's many gods and spirits. Shrines to Dewi Sri, the rice goddess, stand in the flooded fields. Here women are delivering offerings to secure Dewi Sri's blessing on the crop.

SCHOOL DAYS

Education has improved at a rapid rate since Indonesia became a republic. The number of people now able to read has increased dramatically. Girls and boys must attend six years of primary schooling. Secondary education is not yet available everywhere, but the number of girls attending high schools and universities is growing.

SCHOOLING IN INDONESIA		
Age	School	Opportunity
Under 7 years	Preschool	Places for 20 out of 100 children
7–13 years	Primary	Compulsory (free in government schools)
13–15 years	Junior Secondary	Soon to be compulsory
16–18 years	Senior Secondary	Voluntary
Over 18 years	Universities/colleges	Voluntary

In Jakarta, students attend school from 7:00 a.m. until 12:30 p.m., or from 1:00 until 5:30 p.m. State colleges and private universities provide teacher-training programs and other courses. Many Indonesian children learn at least two languages. In some regions, lessons may be given in the local language for the first two years, but after that they are in Bahasa Indonesia. High school students learn English because it is the official foreign language.

▼ Less than twenty percent of children below primary age go to school. Most preschools are privately run and located in the cities.

▶ Children can join a *gamelan* orchestra from an early age. Organizations outside school also teach singing and dancing.

▼ Some young people look for jobs as soon as they leave primary school. But in the crowded cities work is hard to come by. These hat sellers are among the lucky ones.

▲ Country children learn important lessons out of school. They need to be able to control water buffalo before they can help with farming.

AL FAATIHAH (PEMBUKAAN)

SURAT KE 1 : 7 ayat

JUZ 1

1. Dengan menyebut nama Allah Yang Maha Pemurah lagi Maha Penyayang [1]).

2. Segala puji [2]) bagi Allah, Tuhan semesta alam [3]),

3. Maha Pemurah lagi Maha Penyayang.

4. Yang menguasai [4]) hari pembalasan [5]).

▲ Muslim boys and girls must study the *Koran*, the sacred book of Islam. This is hard for them because the *Koran* is written in Arabic.

▲ Trainee dancers learn to bend their bodies and move gracefully.

◀ In government primary schools throughout the archipelago, students wear uniforms. They can choose their own footwear.

VISITING INDONESIA

This book has shown some of the diversity of Indonesia's places, people, and history. Across the archipelago, people today live with echoes from the past. In Bali, for example, farmers tend rice crops in the ancient way and dancers perform stories that are centuries old. But Indonesia is also becoming a modern, industrialized nation, using up-to-date agricultural methods and industrial technology. The country makes the most of its natural resources, such as copper in Irian Jaya and forests in Kalimantan. Visitors to Indonesia can enjoy both old and new. For example, they can watch wooden puppet shows called *wayang golek*, which first came to Indonesia in the fifteenth century, or go scuba diving with the latest underwater equipment.

▲ Horse trekking is an exciting way to see Mount Bromo on East Java. Other challenges for adventurous tourists include caving in East Kalimantan, mountain biking on Lombok, or hang gliding on Bali.

▼ Indonesia has some unusual forms of transport. Horse power is harnessed to draw covered carts

▲ . . . and pedal power is used to drive three-wheeled rickshaws called *becaks*.

▼ Wooden puppets operated by rods.

▶ Indonesia contains many reminders that people have lived here for centuries. This Batak king's grave on Samosir Island in the middle of Lake Toba is a glimpse of ancient history.

INDONESIAN BEHAVIOR

When in Indonesia, try to do as the Indonesians do.

- Indonesians use their left hand for washing themselves. Do not eat, give, or receive objects, or touch people with the left hand.
- Most Indonesians believe that a person's head contains the soul or life force and is therefore sacred. Do not touch anyone on the head or pat the head of a small child.
- Pointing with the index finger is rude in Indonesia. Copy the graceful beckoning gesture with the palm and fingers facing downwards.
- Indonesians think feet are the lowliest part of the body. Do not point with your toes or the tip of your shoe. Remove your shoes when entering a house and never put your feet on a table.
- Indonesians remain outwardly calm when they are angry. They do not raise their voices during arguments and may smile when talking about serious matters. Do not be impatient.
- In Indonesian theater, angry characters fold their arms or stand with their hands on their hips. In real life, Indonesians think such gestures are insulting. Do not use them.

▲ One of the quickest ways to see some of Indonesia's interesting animals is to visit a Javan zoo. But reserves in the archipelago protect wildlife in more natural surroundings. Komodo dragons live on Komodo and small islands nearby. These distant relatives of the dinosaurs are giants among today's lizards.

▼ From this shop you can buy musical instruments, statues, masks, jewelry, or other souvenirs. Most Indonesian shopkeepers expect customers to bargain over prices.

INDEX

How to use the Index
Each subject is listed alphabetically.
Words in standard type are specific references.
Words in **bold** type refer to the subject in general and
may include other word references within the text.